Amazing Animal Facts

Animal Fun Facts to Share with Kids

INTRODUCTION

Animals can be cute, cuddly, fast, smart … and gross, but they're all pretty amazing! Kids love learning about animals, so these amazing animal facts are perfect for sharing with your kids.

Let's get started!!!

THERE ARE AN ESTIMATED 700 MILLION TO 1 BILLION DOGS IN THE WORLD.

AN OSTRICH'S EYES ARE BIGGER THAN ITS BRAIN.

3

BATS ARE THE ONLY MAMMALS THAT CAN FLY!

SOME
HUMMINGBIRDS
WEIGH LESS
THAN A PENNY.

DRAGONFLIES CAN SEE IN ALL DIRECTIONS AT THE SAME TIME.

BATS HAVE THUMBS.

GORILLAS
BURP WHEN
THEY'RE HAPPY!

A GIRAFFE HAS
SEVEN BONES
IN ITS NECK
(THE SAME AS A
HUMAN, BUT THEY
ARE MUCH LARGER).

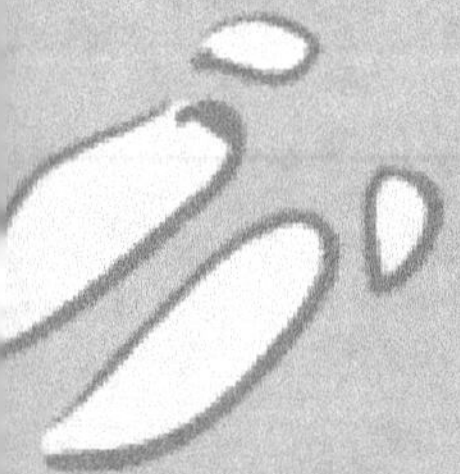

SHARKS LAY THE
BIGGEST EGGS IN
THE WORLD.

CHEETAHS ONLY NEED TO DRINK ONCE EVERY THREE TO FOUR DAYS.

YOU CAN TELL
THE AGE OF A
WHALE BY LOOKING
AT THE WAX PLUG
IN ITS EAR.

GORILLA NOSEPRINTS ARE AS UNIQUE AS HUMAN FINGERPRINTS!

MALE RHINOS ARE
CALLED BULLS,
AND FEMALE
ELEPHANTS ARE
CALLED COWS.

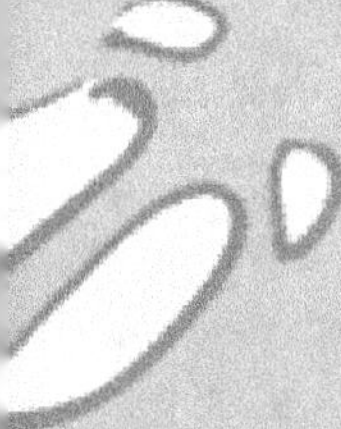

A TIGER'S ROAR CAN BE HEARD AS FAR AS THREE KILOMETERS AWAY.

WALRUSES CAN
SLEEP IN WATER.

GIANT ANTEATERS CAN EAT OVER 30,000 INSECTS A DAY.

STARFISH HAVE NO BRAIN AND NO BLOOD. AND THEY AREN'T EVEN FISH!

BABY ELEPHANTS ARE ABLE TO STAND WITHIN 20 MINUTES OF BEING BORN.

REINDEER GROW
NEW ANTLERS
EVERY YEAR.

SLOTHS ARE SO SLOW THAT IN THEIR NATIVE CLIMATE, ALGAE ACTUALLY GROWS ON THEIR FUR.

SOME LAND SNAILS CAN SLEEP FOR UP TO THREE YEARS IN HIBERNATION OR AESTIVATION.

A GRIZZLY BEAR'S BITE IS SO STRONG THAT IT CAN CRUSH A BOWLING BALL.

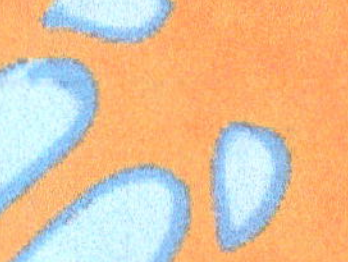

RATS LAUGH
WHEN BEING
TICKLED.

THERE ARE
NO MALE OR
FEMALE
EARTHWORMS.

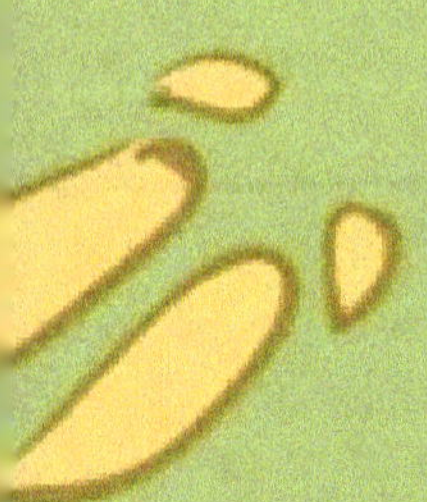

A JAGUAR'S NIGHT VISION IS SIX TIMES BETTER THAN A HUMAN'S.

A HUMMINGBIRD'S WINGS CAN BEAT UP TO 200 TIMES PER SECOND TO HOVER.

VAMPIRE BATS
HAVE SUCH SHARP
TEETH THAT YOU
MAY NOT FEEL
THEM BITE YOU.

HUMANS SHARE 98.8% OF CHIMPANZEE DNA.

A CAT CAN USE
ITS WHISKERS TO
CHECK WHETHER
IT WILL FIT INTO
A SPACE.

A CHAMELEON'S TONGUE CAN BE TWICE AS LONG AS ITS BODY.

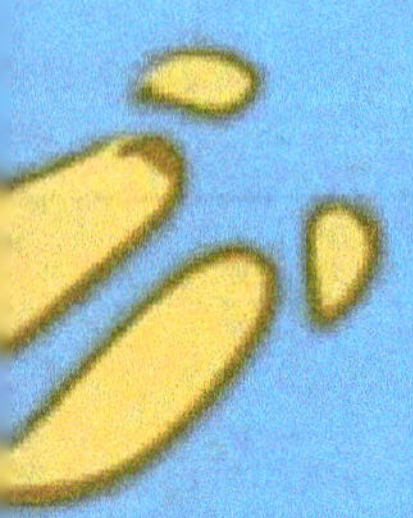

THE HIPPO'S
CLOSEST LIVING
RELATIVES ARE
WHALES,
DOLPHINS, AND
PORPOISES.

ADULT BISON ARE
THE LARGEST
LAND MAMMALS IN
NORTH AMERICA.

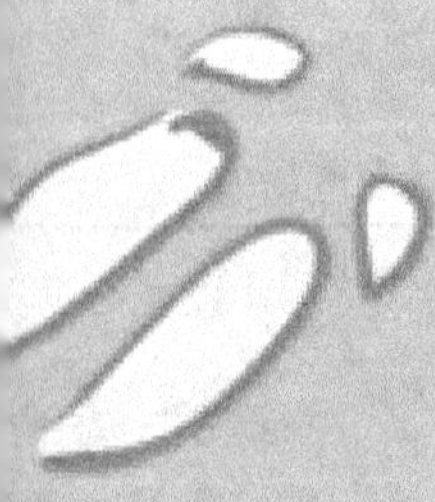

AN EAGLE'S
VISION IS FOUR
TIMES SHARPER
THAN A HUMAN'S.

NINE-BANDED ARMADILLOS ALWAYS GIVE BIRTH TO IDENTICAL QUADRUPLETS.

THE GIANT
TORTOISE OF
THE GALAPAGOS
ISLANDS WEIGHS
AS MUCH AS A
BROWN BEAR.

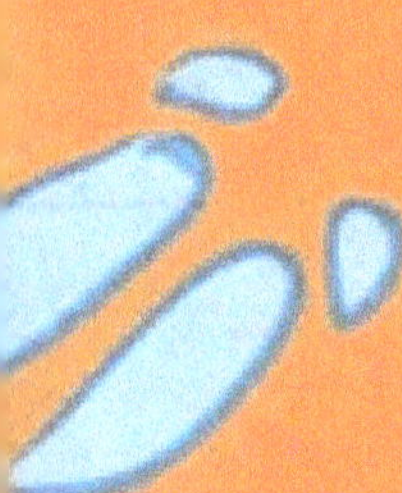

SEA OTTERS HAVE
THE DENSEST FUR
OF ANY MAMMAL.

CAT FLEAS HAVE AMAZING JUMPING SKILLS.

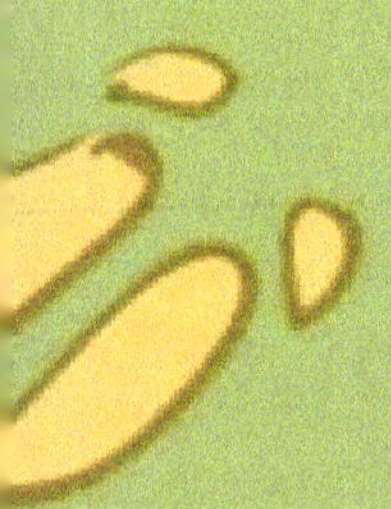

AN EMPEROR
PENGUIN CAN STAY
UNDERWATER FOR
27 MINUTES.

CAMELS CAN DRINK 50 GALLONS OF WATER IN 3 MINUTES.

KIWIS HAVE NOSTRILS AT THE END OF THEIR LONG BEAKS.

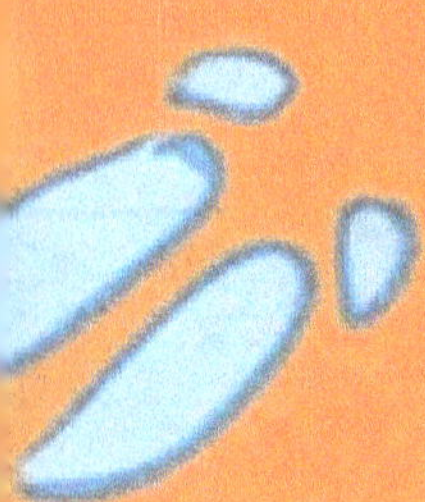

A GROUP OF
FLAMINGOS IS
CALLED A
FLAMBOYANCE.

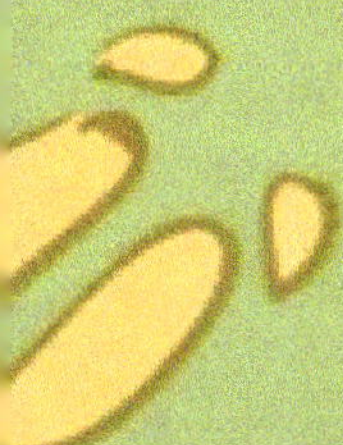

SNAKES CAN SEE WITH THEIR EYES CLOSED.

SHEEP HAVE FOUR STOMACHS.

ONLY FEMALE MOSQUITOS BITE.

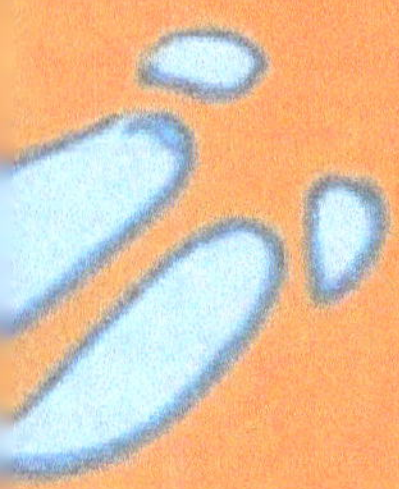

SALAMANDERS CAN REGENERATE BODY PARTS.

KIWIS LAY EGGS THAT CAN WEIGH UP TO A QUARTER OF THEIR BODY WEIGHT.

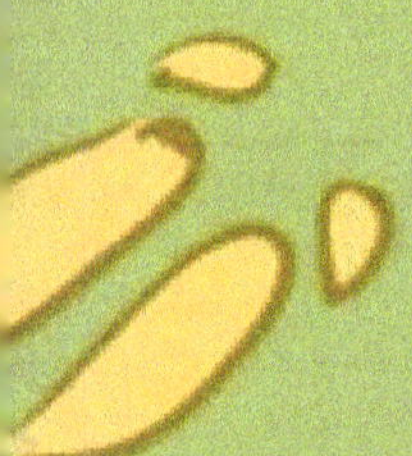

OCTOPUSES HAVE THREE HEARTS AND BLUE BLOOD.

HONEYBEES COMMUNICATE THROUGH DANCE.

ELEPHANTS
CAN SENSE RAIN
UP TO 150 MILES
AWAY.

A GROUP OF CROWS IS CALLED A MURDER.

TURTLES CAN
BREATHE
THROUGH THEIR
BUTTS.

PENGUINS HAVE KNEES INSIDE THEIR BODIES.

LOBSTERS HAVE TEETH IN THEIR STOMACHS.

A SNAIL CAN GROW BACK A NEW EYE IF IT LOSES ONE.

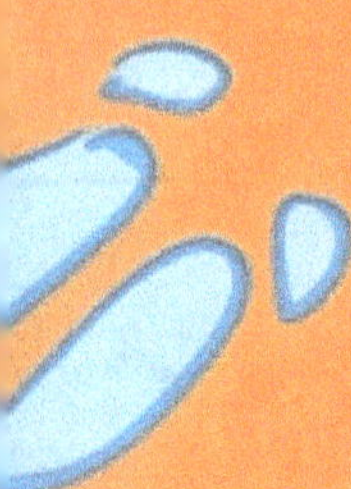

CROCODILES
CAN GALLOP LIKE
HORSES.

BUTTERFLIES TASTE WITH THEIR FEET.

THE CHEETAH IS THE ONLY CAT THAT HAS SEMI-RETRACTABLE CLAWS.

FROGS CAN FREEZE WITHOUT DYING.

GOLDFISH CAN RECOGNIZE FACES.

THE MALE SEAHORSE CARRIES AND GIVES BIRTH TO BABIES.

A COW
GIVES NEARLY
200,000
GLASSES OF MILK
IN ITS LIFETIME.

RAVENS CAN
MIMIC HUMAN
SPEECH AND
OTHER SOUNDS.

THERE ARE NO MOSQUITOES IN ICELAND.

AN ANT CAN LIFT 5,000 TIMES ITS OWN WEIGHT.

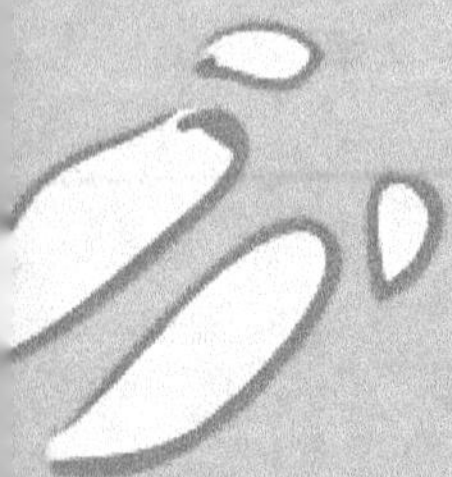

THE LIFESPAN OF A HOUSEFLY IS ONLY 15 TO 25 DAYS.

THE ONLY CONTINENT WITHOUT NATIVE ANTS IS ANTARCTICA.

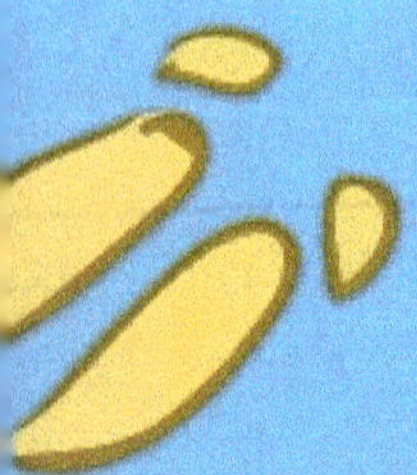

OWLS DON'T HAVE
EYEBALLS, THEY
HAVE EYE TUBES.

THE BASENJI IS THE ONLY DOG THAT CAN'T BARK.

A GROUP OF RHINOS IS CALLED A CRASH.

DOLPHINS SLEEP
WITH ONE EYE
OPEN.

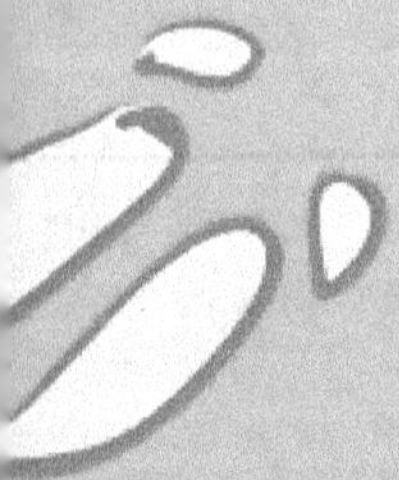

A CAT HAS
32 MUSCLES IN
EACH EAR.

AN ELEPHANT CAN SMELL WATER UP TO 12 MILES AWAY.

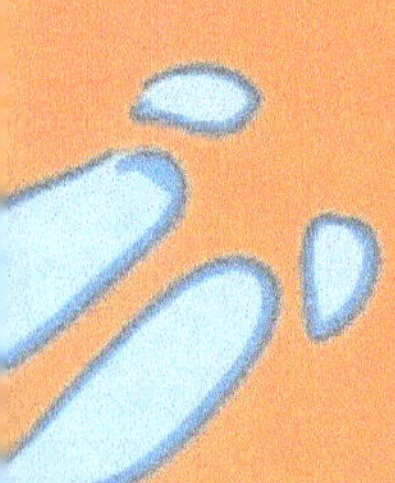

A BUTTERFLY
HAS A LIFESPAN
OF ONLY ABOUT
TWO WEEKS.

THE WORLD'S SMALLEST DOG BREED IS THE CHIHUAHUA.